TOUCHING
THE LIGHT
DAY BY DAY

365

ILLUMINATIONS
TO LIVE BY

Meg Blackburn Losey, Ph.D.

WEISERBOOKS
San Francisco, CA / Newburyport, MA

First published in 2012 by Weiser Books
Red Wheel/Weiser, LLC
With offices at:
665 Third Street, Suite 400
San Francisco, CA 94107
www.redwheelweiser.com

ISBN: 978-1-57863-527-6

Library of Congress Cataloging-in-Publication Data available
upon request

Cover design by www.levanfisherdesign.com/ Barbara Fisher
Interior design by Cody Gates, Happenstance Type-O-Rama

Printed in the United States of America
TS
10 9 8 7 6 5 4 3 2 1

About the Author

Meg Blackburn Losey, Ph.D., is the author of the international bestseller *The Children of Now*. She is also the author of *Parenting the Children of Now*, *The Secret History of Consciousness*, *Touching the Light*, and a contributor to the bestselling *The Mystery of 2012* anthology.

Dr. Meg is the creator/channeler of The Living Light Cards. She is a Master Healer, speaker, and teacher. Dr. Meg is an ordained minister in both Spiritual Science and Metaphysics. She is a Ph.D. of Holistic Life Coaching and holds a Doctoral Degree in Metaphysics. She lives in eastern Washington. Visit her at *www.spiritlite.com*.

To Our Readers

Weiser Books, an imprint of Red Wheel/Weiser, publishes books across the entire spectrum of occult, esoteric, speculative, and New Age subjects. Our mission is to publish quality books that will make a difference in people's lives without advocating any one particular path or field of study. We value the integrity, originality, and depth of knowledge of our authors.

Our readers are our most important resource, and we appreciate your input, suggestions, and ideas about what you would like to see published.

Visit our website at *www.redwheelweiser.com* to learn about our upcoming books and free downloads, and be sure to go to *www.redwheelweiser.com/newsletter/* to sign up for newsletters and exclusive offers.

You can also contact us at *info@redwheelweiser.com* or at

RED WHEEL/WEISER, LLC
665 Third Street, Suite 400
San Francisco, CA 94107

To David

To My Readers ~

Each morning I awaken with a bit of brilliance floating in my awareness, a little illumination that is a sweet reflection of life and often a profound thought for the day. It is as if the Light of Creation has reached deeply into me and brought forward from my slumber the wisdom of the ages. How can I keep them to myself? In sharing these with you, it is my desire to remind you that you are whole and perfect beings of creation, with the ability and the power to create whatever kind of life experience you desire. Let these little thoughts light your way to your greatest joy and all of the perfection that is innate within your very beings!

With love and gratitude,

Meg
Meg Blackburn Losey, Ph.D.

1

A little chaos now and then
serves to shake us out of our
comfortable discomfort.

*I accept that chaos serves to motivate
me even when I don't understand
why it is happening.*

2. Our ability to create reality is directly relative to how strongly and purely we believe in the outcome.

I know that whatever I imagine is already a reality and that the process isn't important as long as I am willing to keep moving toward the outcome.

———

3. Anticipation without expectations leads to excellence of experience without disappointment.

I am willing to ride the wave of creation, allowing it to deliver to me from all its possibilities.

4. Creation is both elegant and eloquent without needing to show off or uttering a word. Look around you . . . everything is a reflection of us.

I accept that I am beautiful inside and out no matter what.

———

5. That deep unconditional love we seek from others lies in the divinity that is us. It isn't something to find, to take, or to have, but rather to be.

I am divine, no matter how imperfect I or others believe me to be. I can be nothing less.

6. Our sensitivity is directly relative to how much we are willing to feel.

I am open to the depths of my soul, willing to feel fully all that life has to offer.

---

7. Time is of the essence means what we do with it matters most.

Putting off what I want in life is no longer acceptable. I choose to apply my time directly toward all that I desire.

---

8. We usually recognize eloquence when the words spoken carry truth.

Today I will listen past the words and into their true meaning.

9. Often what feels ominous to us is simply something we can't comprehend.

This day I won't be afraid of what I don't understand. Instead I will embrace it with all the love my heart has to offer.

———

10. Elegance has many faces and one of them is yours as a being of creation, not only created of light, but reflecting it.

I am an expression of creation's elegance, and I reflect all light because I am that.

11. The intensity and satisfaction of our experiences depends upon our willingness to have them.

Today I am willing to be open to whatever comes; no matter what I think, there is magic in everything.

---

12. Hidden treasures lie just beneath our belief that we don't have any.

I don't have to know what my gifts are to have them. I am unlimited in what I am.

---

13. Intimidation is someone else's idea of getting you to do the right thing.

I don't have to jump through hoops just because someone else thinks I should.

14. Stop. Be still. Listen. Are the voices you hear inside your own head yours or everyone else's telling you who you are and what you want and even what to do?

    This day I am willing to listen deeply to what is hidden inside of me, for it is there that the real truth lies.

    ———

15. Death is inevitable. It is life we must choose in order to have lived at all.

    I will not wait for life to come to me. I embrace life while I move my feet exactly toward all that I wish to experience.

    ———

16. Our dreams remain dreams until we choose to live them.

    I am willing to step beyond the boundaries I have created to live whatever I can imagine.

17

In truth, we are not valued by association, accomplishment, or otherwise; instead, we are valued by our own perceptions. The question is, is it really us keeping score, or the voices in and around us?

What may have happened in the past doesn't matter. It is what I do with now that matters.

18. The intention of an investment is to benefit you in the future. How are your thoughts, words, and actions today going to benefit you later?

Today I will take note of the kinds of sentiments I am expressing, knowing that each of them will come back to me a thousand fold. I choose a positive future filled with only what I really want, not what I fear.

———

19. Sometimes just "winging it" works far better than all the best laid plans.

Today I am willing to be flexible, going with the flow; even when I don't know where I am going, part of me does.

20. Who are we without the mirrors of each other? Only we know who is behind the mask.

When I look past my fears of not being enough, good enough, or deserving, I see myself in everyone around me, and we are beautiful.

———

21. We can blame whomever whenever but ultimately the diligence was ours.

I accept responsibility for all of the choices that I make and have made, and know that when I don't like what I have chosen, I can simply choose again.

———

22. What can't be driven can be finessed.

This day I will stop trying so hard, noticing that sometimes it is the little things I never considered that make huge differences in my life.

23. Free. Will. No one is giving it away ~
we already have it.

*I have the freedom to do or choose whatever
my heart desires in every moment.*

---

24. Intention, undirected, is always a
what if.

*Today I won't just wish, I will act on my wishes
so that they become reality.*

---

25. We are fully adaptable except for our
resistance.

*Today I will say yes. Whatever may have
stopped me in the past no longer matters.*

26. Coming full circle is in one sense completion, in another starting over, and in another Karmic, and yet in it all, an opportunity to start fresh with a clean slate.

I realize that endings make room for new and exciting things to come my way.

———

27. A moment of observation can contribute a lifetime of knowledge.

This day I will slow down and really notice what is happening around me.

———

28. Reality is a field of possibility defined by choice.

Reality isn't happening to me, I am happening to reality! I choose to create all of my desired outcomes by making the choices that are my God given right.

29. Sometimes in chaos while things are moving way too fast, if we don't get emotional or caught up in the craziness, we can begin to see clearly, almost in slow motion, almost in suspended time, the doorways to something different.

Today as I experience what seems to be chaos, I will look closer so that I will recognize opportunities that come my way.

---

30. Create more than you use.

I understand that balance is necessary. Today I agree to give back as much as I receive.

---

31. What if the impossible were just a bunch of possibilities entangled?

I realize that everything is simple and there is no need to complicate anything.

32. Our most intense feelings are our creation, no one else's.

This day I accept that I, and I alone, am responsible for how I feel. No one can change that but me.

---

33. We can only imagine what is possible. Everything is.

I believe that anything I can imagine is already possible, I just need to find the way there.

---

34. Our abilities aren't comparable; they are a package of forward expression that is our unique gift to ourselves and the world.

Who I am is irreplaceable in this world. I am a perfect and mighty being of creation.

35. Loss leaves room for what is yet to come.

I realize that my feelings of emptiness are nothing more than my soul craving to be filled with new and exciting experiences.

———————

36. That deep unconditional love we seek from others lies in the divinity that is us. It isn't something to find, to take, or to have, but rather to be.

I choose to step into the world today with a sense of complete fullness. From there, all of my experiences will be enhanced because there is no room for anything else.

———————

37. Our Spirit is Mighty. Our Enemy is our Fear.

Today I embrace all of my vulnerabilities as aspects of my perfection.

38. If we imagine and believe something to be so, the reality already exists, and there will be a moment in time when we and our reality intersect.

I know without a doubt that if I wish to create something in my life, it is already so.

---

39. As we know ourselves we will know all others.

Today I choose to share compassion with myself so that I can feel more deeply in all of my relationships.

40

Our attention often gets so focused on the process that we forget the intended outcome.

This day I realize that whatever I imagine, so it is.

41. Surrender implies defeat. Humility
allows for all possibilities.

*When I let down all of my defenses I become a
living possibility.*

———

42. A lifetime only seems that way when we
are looking for what we think we don't
have.

*What I have been waiting for wasn't realistic.
Now it is. This day I realize that I have all that I
need and that perhaps what I thought I needed
was fear trying to fill me with distractions.*

43. Good directions are only a suggestion. Free will determines the final route.

Today I won't waver from my intended route unless I decide to do so.

———

44. What is wild may not be really so, instead just free of self-imposed encumbrances.

Today I will let myself out of the cage and freely express myself with ease and grace remembering that I don't have to hurt anyone to tell the truth.

45. The strength of our ability to move beyond the mundane is dependent upon our courage to do so.

I embrace every moment with great courage and gentleness of heart, never looking back or forward, shining in this now.

---

46. Seek not to follow others away from your true destination, for it is there, all the time, within you.

Even when my mind doubts me, my soul knows the way.

---

47. The mark of true intelligence is the wisdom that silently guides it.

This day I will not cover my true intentions with excuses or words; instead, I will listen deeply to the GPS of my soul.

48. Feeling intense means we have left our comfort zone . . . finally!

Today if I feel anxious I will celebrate myself for having leaped into new possibilities.

———

49. What we defend about ourselves was never real in the first place.

I realize that if I need to shield myself maybe I need to look more honestly at what I am defending.

———

50. We can hit any target with intention, forethought, concentration, and a steady aim.

Today I will remain true to what I have conceived possible, because since it is my creation, I know I can't miss.

51. Jealousy is like having an incurable illness and waiting desperately for someone else to die from it.

This day I realize that the experiences I am having are exactly mine, and as full as I am, I have no need for concern about what others have that is different.

———

52. Our perceptions are only as great as our willingness to imagine.

Today I am willing to consider that anything is possible only when I am willing to imagine it.

53. Sometimes when we are caught in the illusion, the greatest destructive forces are hidden in the most joyous of experiences.

Today I will be especially truthful with myself, being willing to accept truths that maybe I didn't want but that serve to pave the way for what I do want.

———

54. Self-sabotage is our way of saying we aren't worth it.

This day I accept that I am worth it, deserving, willing and grateful to have or experience all that I aspire toward.

55. How high we can fly is completely dependent upon our willingness to take off.

Today I realize that no one is keeping score and that nothing limits me when it comes to experiencing fullness in my life.

———

56. There is no real meaning in words, only in the spaces between them.

Today I will become an observer, noticing truth beyond words and allowing that truth to reveal itself to me as it will.

57. One oops is worth a thousand laughs . . .
or a lifetime of regret ∽ our choice.

Today I will laugh at myself every chance I get.

---

58. How hard we work trying to fix things
that aren't broken!

*I will only embrace what is mine to carry. All
else I release with relief and gratitude that it
isn't mine to lug around.*

59

When we have our minds on
what was, we miss what is.

*I realize that what has passed was.
What is now is the key to all else.*

60. The need of the ego to falsely define greatness comes from its learned sense of insignificance.

This day I refuse to accept from anyone any-where anything that states or implies that I am anything less than perfect.

———

61. Interior development means exterior gain.

Today I will get to know myself, learning what I really want and shedding all that I do not.

———

62. We are obscured by our ego's sense of greatness.

I realize that being vulnerable is not only OK, it reveals my true self and therefore everyone else's too.

63. A prayer is only as powerful as the passion behind it.

Today I won't beg when I say my prayers. I will command with the force of creation all that I know can be true, that it is I who decides my own fate.

———

64. If we were books what would be our content? Would our stories make sense? Do they?

I realize that my life's story is an ongoing masterpiece that I create because I choose it to be so, and the challenges in my story can have any outcome I create.

65. While it is validating, evidence of our achievements isn't necessary for us to know we have succeeded. There is no score to keep, no judges hovering over us but ourselves and our very best in every given moment. How can we lose?

This day I let go of all need to achieve and instead embrace the opportunity to live in every now as if it were the only one there ever would be.

———

66. The value of what we hold onto is questionable.

I realize that what doesn't serve me is holding me back from what does.

67. We can wonder about life, speculate, doubt, question, or even be unsure of our journey, or, we can wonder, be in awe, marvel, and, yes, even be astonished at all of the perfection around us.

This day I free the child in me to wonder at everything I encounter.

———————

68. Instant gratification is all about filling a hole that never existed in the first place.

Today I let go of my need to feel secure by needing instant results. I understand that creation is working diligently to provide me with what is exactly perfect.

69. When we feel insignificant, it is because we haven't recognized ourselves.

When I see myself in any light today, I will witness my own splendor in relation to all other things.

———

70. When we "handle" things, we interfere with their natural unfolding.

This day I let go of my need to control all outcomes, knowing that all is already created in perfect light.

71. What we believe, we have learned. What we know is truth. What we know is our unlimited consciousness bringing back to our limited world all that is immeasurable, infinite, and pure. What our minds do with that is a travesty. Trust what you know.

   I really get it that I not only don't have to understand everything in life, I can't possibly. Today I agree to let things be as they are.

---

72. The only way a door will open is if we walk toward it and turn the handle.

   Today I will not give away my power; instead I will step firmly in whatever direction I choose because I know it is perfect, and no one knows this better than me.

73. The walls we construct will withstand our imagined enemies as well as our worst enemy ~ ourselves ~ and restrict the depth of all our relationships. They are unnecessary.

This day I relax into my easiest being, willing to feel deeply and to love willingly all that comes my way.

———

74. Sentience: The ability to feel and respond with feeling. We sense with our entire being, with our energy fields and our bodies as a whole. When we are present in the now, we become aware of the more subtle things we are picking up and can respond rather than react.

In this now there is more going on in me than I can possibly grasp. I accept that that is OK and that I don't always have to know everything.

75. Life isn't a contract to be fulfilled, or a purpose to be sought. It is for living, pure and simple, unobstructed by guilt or grief or anything else that can take away our joy. Live largely, loudly, and lightly!

Today I choose to live out loud with joy and lack of inhibition.

---

76. Satisfaction is a platform for expansion. If we are constantly looking for something better, we are never satisfied and therefore remain in need.

My light shines brightly through all obstacles, showing me the way toward my greatest desires. It is up to me to walk in my own light.

77. Value is a perspective that we tie to all things external but forget to apply internally first. If we did, everything would look different, and all of our perceptions would have an entirely new system of discernment.

I am not only valuable, I am priceless, irreplaceable in every way. I deserve whatever I want and need and am open to receiving it all with gratitude.

———

78. Loneliness is lessened when we are comfortable with our own company.

No one can fill me because I am filled with the unconditional love of my source. Instead, I accept all that I know: that I and all whom I encounter can only augment each other.

79. A gentle touch, a hug, a kind word can change not only someone's day, but their entire life.

Today I will reach outward toward others with loving kindness and compassion, particularly when I don't want to.

---

80. Our need to be logical is our greatest detriment. There is so much beyond what our brains can comprehend that we often miss the subtleties while trying to understand. When we can relax our defenses we are completely available to ourselves and therefore all else.

Today I release the need to know or understand anything, allowing myself to free flow without needing to know where I am going.

81. An expectation is a disappointment waiting to happen.

This day I realize that no one has a clue what I expect of them and therefore can't please me. Instead, I open to everything others might contribute to my day and I to theirs.

---

82. Every circumstance is lined with motivations . . . ours, and those of others. The important thing to focus on is ours. What others intend really has nothing to do with us unless we follow their intentions instead of our own, and that rarely works.

Why no longer matters, nor does how or when or where; just that I am is all that I need to be and others will follow me there.

83

Life's lessons are not punishment for anything we have done wrong. They are opportunities we give ourselves to expand our awareness and make different choices next time.

Today, instead of resisting my disappointments, I will celebrate them as opportunities that will bring me far more than any mistake ever could have.

84. Greatness does not come from a need to be so, it comes from focus of purpose, integrity of self, the courage to stand alone when all others have fled, the knowing that in spite of all others' doubts, the chosen path is unquestionably certain and the humility not to notice that all of the above are even taking place.

I am a great and mighty spirit. In this now I am at the peak of my being and I am brilliant. I don't need to tell anyone else because I am self-evident.

---

85. Being invisible does not protect us; it delays, if not stifles, the realization of our dreams and keeps us limited from the experiences that would have come our way if anyone had noticed us.

I realize that being seen doesn't have to mean exposure, but instead recognition.

86. Anger is not usually about what is happening in a certain moment but what we couldn't help in moments past.

Today I will see my emotions for the truth they reveal, not needing to subject anyone else to whatever frustrations I may not have yet recognized.

———

87. Unconditional love isn't co-dependent upon anything or anyone. It is a power generated by the spirit and is a way of being, not a singular act.

This day I become the center of my own grace, radiating it outward from the depths of who I am.

88. The question isn't if we live a long life, but if we choose to live it at all.

This day if I don't like the outcome of my choices I will definitely choose again.

———

89. No challenge can be a success without effort.

I realize that I don't grow unless I stretch beyond what I know. Today I will grow like a wildfire, accepting challenges as fuel to the fire of my being.

———

90. Having experience doesn't make us wise or smart; it is what we do with the experience that does.

I realize that who I am is my life's work and that I am a constantly evolving being whose wisdom is embodied in my actions, my words and my thoughts. It is that which I wish to share today.

91. Even when we don't realize it, we leave an indelible impression on everything, everyone, and everywhere that we touch and encounter. We must be intentional in all of our being, knowing that even when not aware, we have touched every aspect of creation with our essence.

What I choose to leave behind is not the refuse of unwanted experiences but instead, seeds of infinite possibilities.

———

92. Resistance means always having to wonder if only . . .

This day I will not wonder but instead be whatever it is I am aiming for.

93. To trust means not to be afraid.

No one can hurt me unless I decide I want to be in pain. I trust that my soul is safe in every choice it makes and in every hand that I place it.

---

94. Evidence is not necessary to prove truth. Truth is.

What is true to me may not be true to anyone else but that is just fine.

---

95. To live well and full is to expose one's vulnerabilities so that they can become strengths.

Today I will show the world my soul, that it lights the way for all of us to share the immensity of being. There will be no pain, only love emanating from the joy in my heart.

96

Faith and passion are the fuel for perfect completion of any intention.

Today I trust that all is as it would be, that what I have intended will be so.

97. Panic is a case of the "can't help its" that comes on when we don't have an immediate solution. When we take a moment and breathe, we find that there are always solutions and that we can help it!

Today I grasp that my moments of panic are all about seeing myself as something less than I am. I realize the truth of my greatness and stand firmly in my infinite roots, strong and true.

———

98. While revenge may seem sweet in the moment, its aftereffects, as our act ripples outward then back again, can come back to bite us. What seemed sweet in its moment can become toxic to us.

Everything I do, every energy that I expend, whether in words, thoughts, or actions, is an investment in my future. I choose to invest only in what enhances my life experience.

99. Innocence isn't childishness or ignorance or naivety. Innocence is authenticity, being undefended from the purest of joys and leading from the heart.

Today my heart leaps with joy in everything I encounter, and I will wonder at the exquisiteness of it all.

———

100. Nothing is a simple matter of fact. There are always unseen, unknown aspects to every situation.

I realize that everything is intricately woven into the greater One and that all things are as simple as I let them be.

———

101. Benevolence is not for self gain.

To truly give a gift is to have no need of experiencing the recipient's satisfaction. The true satisfaction is in having done the deed.

102. Dissonance is more than lack of reso-
nance. It is lack of honest awareness
that inner balance has gone awry.

*As I find myself feeling out of harmony with
others or my surroundings, I will look deeply
within myself to find the truth of my feelings.
Are they mine or something else?*

―――――

103. In order to go with the flow we must
remain fluid.

*As I go about my day I will remember that
nothing is written in stone and that being
flexible, willing to go with changes as they
occur, will take me to my intended destination
much more quickly and peacefully.*

104. What is manifest is an expression of creation displaying the reality we have imagined. We are that. It is us. We are the consciousness within the living One, directing its creative efforts toward the manifestation of our consciousness as reality . . .

Today I choose to see myself in everyone and everything around me. I will look for the beauty of us everywhere.

---

105. Inspiration comes from considering new and different possibilities.

I will joyfully step out of my comfort zone today to consider new possibilities and embrace them fully.

106. Gratitude is the grease that keeps the wheel of good fortune turning.

Today I am grateful for all that I am, all that is mine, and all that I will have and encounter throughout every moment.

------

107. To be indispensible means that no one can do without you. The real question is, can you do without them?

Today I will ask for help, and then I will allow the resulting assistance with ease.

------

108. Necessity is relative to need, but consider the fact that the need may or may not be real.

This day I will consider the fact that I need far less than I think I do, and that I am fulfilled by the light of creation, leaving no room for emptiness of any kind.

109. Manifestation is clarity of intent personified.

I am a powerful creator of all that I desire and all that I need, and I deserve it.

———

110. Absolution comes with the realization that a sin never occurred; a choice was made and we did the best we could.

This day I forgive all that has caused me pain, knowing that it was me who chose to feel what I have felt, and who now chooses peace. I am forgiven for all that I believed I failed.

111

The amount of abundance we
have is directly relative to how
much we value ourselves.

*Today I accept that I am a priceless
being of creation and that it is impossible that I could be anything less.*

112. Success has everything to do with out-comes and little to do with the process.

Whatever I do today will be a success, I have no need to worry or fear about my perfor-mance. All I need to do is the best that I can.

———

113. Excellence comes from one part inspi-ration, two parts willingness, three parts imagination, and acting faithfully without limitation toward an intended outcome that becomes everything we knew that it could.

Today I acknowledge that I am living, breath-ing excellence, a reflection of my Creator, an aspect of the living One. I can be nothing less.

114. Bliss does not have to be relative.

In this now I choose Joy, I will live it,
breathe it, feel it, express it, dance with it,
and embody it as I am filled, because I can.

———

115. If we are already perfection, then why
do we work so hard to be anything else?

Today I realize that there is nothing to heal
and everything to love about me.

116. Whatever destination you have set is a journey that begins and ends with you. It is a travel of your imaginings that has no boundaries except those which you alone place in your road.

I am the creator of my journey, I choose of my own free will, allowing nothing to stand in my way, or take away the joy I find in every turn. I am my own light.

———

117. Innuendoes are truths without courage.

When I feel critical today, I will look again, noticing what I love about what I wanted to loathe.

118. Excellence comes when there is no
consideration for anything less.

*That I am excellence leaves room for nothing
else. I am a spirit walking the earth, remembering my perfection and because of that I
can't do anything but shine.*

———

119. Nothing is possible until we are aware
that it is.

*This day I am willing to consider the ideas of
others that they may trigger something in me
that is vitally new and therefore attainable.*

120. Being reasonable can be the most unreasonable thing to do.

Today when I want to argue with someone, I will look again beyond their words and actions to find the true motivation behind why my buttons just got pushed.

———

121. Sometimes a thought does not need to be expressed but instead let go into the ethers, as its pure form is greater than a thousand words.

Power follows thought. I am the power behind my own experiences. I am great beyond my imaginings.

122. The ability to be honest is one of our inherent gifts.

Today I will be honest with myself until I can do it without hurting myself or anyone else.

———

123. When we feel the need to say we are not being judgmental, perhaps we are after all.

Today I will realize that I gain no value at the expense of others because as I criticize them, I hurt me too.

———

124. Sometimes we need exactly the opposite of what we crave.

This day before I leap into an impulsive anything, I will consider if it is really what I want.

125. Paradox: When two opposites clash with no apparent solution or compromise. Is the battle worth the effort?

Today I don't have to be right, I just have to be who I am and that is just fine.

――――――

126. What if we realized that we are already what we were trying to be?

Today I will see myself through the eyes of my source, and I will realize that I am perfect in every way, that all else is merely the opinion of others and they aren't living my life for me.

127. Mistakes don't happen: Guilt does.
When we realize that our mistakes are
only opportunities to do something
different, the guilt has nowhere to go
but disappear.

My heart has no room for shame or guilt.
Today instead of telling myself I should
have, could have, or would have, I will
laugh instead.

———

128. Everything we ever let go of is full of
claw marks.

The truth is that I need to hold on to nothing,
for if it is truly mine, it will stay until our time
is done, and once it is, I will gratefully send it
on its way.

129. What if we stopped saying what if and started realizing what is?

There is only ever this now. What was, was, and what might be is only my idea of limiting what I can have. In this now I am safe, and I have everything that I need.

―――――

130. All change begins with a single shift in perception.

Today I will see with new eyes all that is in and around me, and I will choose my direction as my light shines solely upon the most perfect path.

131. When we can be still we are no longer avoiding ourselves.

This day, rather than avoiding what I don't understand or what makes me uncomfortable, I will be quietly present, living lifetimes within me and knowing that all is perfection even now.

----

132. When we observe beauty and it touches us, we have found the same in ourselves.

As I look around me I find reflections of my heart, my soul, reminding me that I can be nothing less than the beauty that frees my inner grace.

133

Frustration is our resistance to consider an alternative path.

If I don't know how, can't understand why, think I need to know, I will look upon those moments as keys to doors that will open easily for me, revealing what I had hoped was there all along but was too stubborn to see.

134. Every expression of energy that we make, whether a thought, a word, motion, emotion, anything at all, travels throughout creation infinitely carrying the message of the moment of expression forever. Creation responds by delivering our message back to us as reality.

I choose to live intentionally, being aware that everything that I am and do will touch others, and they me, forever.

---

135. The problem with expectations is that no one but us knows what they are.

This day I will communicate what is in my heart. I will do so with ease and grace, and I will remain safe, even when my deepest feelings are revealed.

136. What is really amazing is that we have the capability to be amazed!

I don't have to be in charge of anything today. I have nothing to protect and everything to experience. Today I choose the freedom to just be.

---

137. Energy, when directed without emotion, is like a shotgun approach to creation. But when we combine our emotion with passion and an intention, the energy refines to a direct connection within creation to effectively bring us everything we were meant to have.

I am the master of all my creations. I depend upon no one to deliver my dreams. Instead I take charge by letting go so that all that I desire can come to me unhindered and far more perfect that I ever could have imagined.

138. We are created equally of all things. All things are created of us. We are not a duality. Instead, we are living light, integral aspects of the living One.

The marriage of my humanity and my divinity is all I ever needed to realize in order for me to walk this earth as a joyful expression of all that has ever been. I am the light of my world and the world of others, too.

———

139. Mysteries remain so when we do not choose to explore them.

Today I choose to step out of what is familiar and into the excitement of new and different. When it is dark, I will look through new eyes, only to realize that I had already arrived and simply forgotten to turn on the light.

140. The immensity of everything is only as big as we make it.

This day I refuse to let drama and trauma override my possibilities.

———

141. We are everything that we believe and nothing that we are told.

I cannot be what others believe me to be, only who I have always been and who I am becoming.

———

142. When we criticize, it is only because someone has mirrored to us something that we have chosen not to recognize in ourselves.

Today instead of blaming someone else I will realize that every situation is my own experience and therefore can't possibly be anyone else's fault. It is I and I alone who embodies all of my perceptions; therefore I am them.

143. Indecision is the same as no decision at all.

Today I will be impulsive, deciding on the spot about what comes in each moment. I will make decisions I have been putting off and I won't look back.

---

144. Sometimes what feels like insanity is brilliance breaking through.

It is okay if I have ideas that are different than everyone else's. After all, the world has been built on inspiration.

145. Our inner child learned to fear and continues to tell us to be afraid. The problem is that the child never realized that the monsters under the bed aren't real and neither are the ones in the closet.

Today I will let my inner child out to play, to discover with innocent eyes what I may have otherwise never seen.

---

146. Patience is not a virtue when it is used as an excuse for not acting on our own behalf.

This day I put to rest all excuses for my pro-crastination. I realize that those excuses were quiet delays to keep me from succeeding and to keep me stranded in a disconnected now. I celebrate my ability to change gears and go with the speed of my thoughts.

147. The immensity of reality can always be refined to the simplicity of a moment.

This day I will find my passion, realizing that it is nothing more than my own love in action.

———

148. There is nothing to heal. We are perfect. It is only our perception that tells us otherwise, and that was taught to us.

I came into this world a miracle of life, perfect in every respect. I haven't changed, only learned to see myself through the critical eyes of others. Knowing this, I realize that I am still the miracle, perfect in every respect, and I will live as I have been born, an empty canvas of possibilities on which I will color my world.

149. We can only be heard if we are willing to be seen.

I can only be seen if I love out loud. It is OK for others to notice me. What I have to say is valuable!

———

150. Be sure that when you think you can't it is actually your own voice telling you and not someone else's.

Today no one is keeping score. I have to be nothing except my perfect self and accomplish only what feels right for me.

151. Sometimes we just have to go for it.

Today I will leap into the unknown, for it is there that all of my answers are, and my dreams are waiting to be real.

———

152. What if we put all of the energy we spend worrying about what we don't want into what we DO want? Imagine!

I have nothing to worry about. All that comes now and in the future I have laid out in splendor to embody as I see fit.

153. The only way to battle untruth is with unequivocal truth.

Today I choose not to conflict but rather to embody the truth that I am. What is not true will simply flow by me, leaving me unscathed.

———

154. We only experience magic when we believe in it.

This day I will find the magic within me. It lies in my heart, waiting to come out and play.

155. Pleasure is an inner smile ~ don't keep it a secret.

Today I will show my pleasure, wearing it in the twinkle of my eyes, the kindness of my words, and the results of all my actions. I will laugh out loud and my laughter will be contagious.

---

156. Wisdom is not some esoteric achievement to strive for. The epitome of wisdom comes when we no longer need to know because we have embodied, become, and live as the true meaning of the knowledge we thought we needed.

This day I have found that true wisdom is often in the silence, revealed in my observations, transformed in my heart, and expressed as compassion and allowance toward all those around me but most of all to myself.

157. Our circumstances do not dictate our experiences ~ we dictate our circumstances.

I command this day all that I desire, all that I need, and embrace it willingly, with grace, and the satisfaction of knowing that I am the creator of my own reality.

---

158. Our logical brains are chronic liars.

Today when I catch myself trying to think my way out of a situation or attempting to justify anything, I will be still and listen to the truth that is within me.

159

How can we believe we are limited creatures when we are infused with the infinite?

I am a true light wrought from the exquisiteness of creation, forged in the fire of infinite brightness, and strengthened by my own convictions.

160. Innocence is not ignorance; it is about seeing clearly and purely with the eyes of the heart.

When I choose to embrace my inner child, I am not weak, but powerful enough to be who I am and be fine in the embodiment of my innocence.

---

161. Confusion is a result of the absence of perceptible or cohesive facts. We cannot discern what we do not know, but we can avoid the drama confusion brings by observing the situation until it makes enough sense for us to discern.

This day I will quietly pay attention to everyone and everything around me, and I will know what is right and true.

162. Gratitude creates an energy exchange that changes our experience from taking to receiving.

I am grateful for all that comes my way, for all that I run to and all that creation has to offer me. I am grateful to be alive to experience the wonders of it all.

————

163. Stillness only comes when we stop running from ourselves.

Today I will find at least ten things about me that I love. Then I will find ten more. Then I will find . . .

164. If we believe we are broken then we must be.

I realize that there is nothing broken about me; I am simply a perfect human being who doesn't need to fit in, but shines brilliantly just as I am.

———

165. Language is the last frontier of communication. We do it first with creation, then energetically through our system, next to our thoughts, and by the time we speak, the message is old news, yet we are still surprised.

Today I have no need to reflexively make words to fill the silence or in my defense. Instead, today I choose to listen deeply and with honor to what others have to say.

166. The result of chaos is magnificence.

Today when I feel the chaos around me, even within me, I will celebrate it, for chaos is the impetus of me stepping forward into exactly what I meant to do, and what I find there will be perfect.

————

167. Ecstasy is us unbridled.

This day I will find deep within me a cosmic, "yeeee-haw, bring it on!"

————

168. The easiest way to sabotage ourselves into disappointment is to have expectations no one else knows about.

Today I will expect nothing.

169. Resistance is our way of saying I don't know how.

It doesn't matter whether I know how or not. What matters is that I am willing to learn whatever it is I need to know.

———

170. Sometimes when we most doubt ourselves we are the most right.

Next time when I say, "I knew it!" it won't be because I regret that I didn't act on something. It will be because I acted on my intuitions today, trusting that I always know more than I realize.

171. Too much stress means that we are doing too much of what everyone else wants and not enough of what we want.

I will listen carefully to what my body is telling me because it is always right. While doing so, I will be willing not only to admit the truth my body reveals, but to act on that truth no matter what.

———

172. Life can't go on without us.

This day I will move forward into new and positive directions. I will lovingly participate in each of my experiences because no one will bring me anything that I can't deliver to myself, and I am worth it.

173. Affirmations only tell us what we already know. We know who we are. We know what we want. Why not just go there and stop repeating ourselves?

Affirmations only tell us what we already know. We know who we are. We know what we want. Why not just go there and stop repeating ourselves?

––––––

174. Synchronicities are always with us, but they are only available when we are present enough to notice them.

Today I choose to notice all of the little things that are happening in every now. I realize that to do so I must fully embody every now, being willing to feel, to express, and to act on whatever I find there.

175. Self-mastery only comes when we no longer have anything to defend, control, criticize, or judge . . . including ourselves!

I accept that I am now and have always been the Master of my Destiny.

---

176. What we hide from ourselves is far greater than what we fear others might see.

This day I realize that what I thought were my detrimental attributes were only fears nipping at me as the voices of those I chose to believe; perhaps they are positive attributes that I had hidden from myself. I care deeply about myself and am willing to look beyond the fears and into my own light.

177

The best of being comes from our being our best at being, not from waiting for someone else to tell us how to be.

I choose my identity, my direction, and even my worth. I choose perfection, perfection, and perfection.

178. Patience may often be a virtue but sometimes it is an excuse for not acting on something when we could have.

Today I will trade procrastination for action, joyfully tending to myself and all that I desire.

---

179. We don't have to do everything alone. It is okay to ask for help and to accept it too.

Today I will not only ask for, but also joyfully accept, all of the assistance that I need without hesitation.

---

180. An edited life isn't much fun. Live largely.

The art of living out loud originates with honesty to myself, coupled with honesty to others, and a lack of hesitation to speak my heart with love.

181. It is impossible to be empty when we are filled with infinite possibilities.

In this now I realize that I no longer have a need to fill myself with things and stuff, but rather with the grace that I am and the recognition of all of the possibilities that are available to me.

---

182. Denial means never having to say I AM.

No matter what come to me this day, I will face it boldly, with an open heart, accepting what is mine and letting what is not reside elsewhere.

183. Discernment means knowing what is best for ourselves in spite of what everyone else believes.

I know what is best for me, and nothing anyone else says or believes needs to be my truth. I will make my own choices based upon what I feel is right for me in every now.

————

184. Yes is a magic word (and so is No).

This day, "Yes!" will be my response to all creation. I am willing to experience what life has to offer, and when an opportunity comes along that I don't want, it is okay for me to say no instead.

185. Saying maybe avoids commitment to self far more than to others. Be direct.

This day I will make commitments that I will keep even if they require effort on my part. I will make choices in the moment, living them so that I never have to look back again.

---

186. Godliness isn't something that only other people have.

I am an aspect of God, created in the image of my source, directly relative to everyone and everything, and because of that, there is nothing I can't do, or have, or be.

187. Innocence does not allow for cynicism.

Today when I find myself doubting, not believing, or just plain negative, I will look again with the eyes of my heart for what it is in me that wants to fight, and I will choose peace instead.

————

188. Mindlessness leads to consciousness.

I don't have to understand everything because that is impossible; instead I choose to trust that which I can't comprehend.

189. Life can be a nugget of satisfaction once in a while, or it can be a feast. This has nothing to do with our appetites and everything to do with our willingness to be the life of the party.

Today I am not holding back. I choose to embrace my life and all that it entails, fully, completely, and without reservation.

————

190. The light of tomorrow's events resides in our expressions of being today.

This day I will be more intentional in my words and acts, knowing that every expression I make dictates tomorrow's experiences.

191. The collective face of humanity is the many-faceted face of God. How do we look? What do we see? And are we revealing and demonstrating the perfection within us, or are we waiting for someone else to get it right?

Today I let go of my reservations, criticisms, and judgments of others, choosing instead compassion for all that I see in them, for they are me and I, them.

---

192. The sweetness of life has many flavors. Try them all.

Today I will try something new, I will do something different, I will encounter new people, and I will relish each experience as an intricate part of the fullness I am creating in me.

193. Wisdom isn't something we learn; it is what we become.

I will embody my experiences, my percep-tions, my thoughts, my heart, all in the truth I know to be evident without any attachment to what things might mean.

---

194. Fear isn't a reality; it is a what if.

When I am afraid, I am leaning into the future for trouble that doesn't exist. I choose now.

195. Grace knows where to go; we just need to let it flow.

This day I will not try to be so specific in my imaginings; rather, I will imagine how I will feel when I have reached the goal I am setting. That way, creation can work with me from its infinite possibilities to bring me far greater results than I could have imagined.

---

196. Lacking trust is our way of keeping things we don't know how to handle at bay.

This day I let down my guard without fear, joyfully embracing what comes, and giving it a chance to show me a different way.

197. Reason is subjective.

This day my mind is at rest. I don't need to figure anything out. I am free of my own delays, and I leap into consideration of new possibilities.

———

198. Discernment allows for clarification of fact over illusion.

This day I set aside all of the untruths I tell myself every day so that I feel special. I am that in spite of me. Today I will look at the truth in all of my life situations, willing to recognize where I have created illusions. I am willing to act toward changing those illusions into truths that serve me well.

199. There are no mistakes, only opportunities to do something different next time.

Today when I screw up, I am going to laugh out loud and then start over again. I cannot make a mistake, only create opportunities for myself to do things differently the next time.

---

200. We have only reached balance when our insides and our outsides feel the same.

Today I am the observer. I am witness to the depths of my feelings. I will assess how I feel inside and how life around me feels too. If my insides do not feel the same as my outside life, I will look truthfully at whatever in me is creating the conflict and change it.

201. When we feel we must dominate another, the only real relationship we are having is with ourselves.

I am created of all things. All things are created of me. Because of that there is nothing and no one who can possibly be lesser or greater than me. I am a child of the living One.

———

202. Value reaches our bank accounts only when we have applied it to ourselves first.

This day I will make a list of everything positive I can think of about me . . . and I will believe it.

203

If we live to work, we are consumed. If we work to live, the quality of our lives becomes much greater and work is no longer our primary goal.

Everything I do today at work will be within the boundaries I have set so that I have time for me no matter what.

204. Power is a perception that is (unfortunately) more often applied to others than to self.

I realize that no one is anymore powerful than me; they just have different agendas and motivations. I don't have to be the pawn of someone else's success.

----

205. True power is gentle power. It is not the power of aggression but rather of the heart reaching forward for what is rightfully hers.

I don't have to fear conflict, nor do I have to participate in it. My heart knows what is true for me, and it is there my loyalty remains without divergence.

206. Look again at the obvious. It isn't what you think.

Today I will observe everything around me, realizing that what I had seen before was my mind telling me how to be safe. As I revisit everything around me, I see that there are abundant opportunities, fellow human beings in every state of their own being, and I in my grace.

---

207. Tolerance is overrated.

I don't have to put up with anything from anyone to be who I am or for them to love and accept me. All I need to do is stay honest with me, and therefore everyone else.

208. When we know ourselves intimately, to even the deepest of places, and accept who we are, then our secrets from ourselves are gone, leaving nothing inside of us that anyone else can hurt.

I will no longer run from what I didn't face in the past. What has been was. I won't worry about what might be because it isn't real. I want to know me to the very depths of my being, for it is there that everything I want, need, imagine, am, resides.

———

209. Being satisfied means letting go of perceptions of lack.

I know now that what I thought I needed was just me trying to fill a place inside of me that I thought was empty. When I look again, there is nothing that I need and everything to experience.

210. Saving something for a special later keeps us from the realization that now is special too.

Now is the most special moment in my life. I celebrate this now with my best of everything!

———

211. Gratitude keeps open the flow of abundance.

I am grateful for all of the little things that touch me in every now, and all of the great gifts that come my way and for all that life has to offer. I accept.

212. We must mind our own spiritual business.

There is no comparison of my intuition, my knowings, or my innate giftedness to that of any other person. I am unique and priceless in every way. What I know is what only I can.

———

213. We are most fulfilled when we recognize our own successes and don't depend upon anyone else to recognize them for us.

What I achieve this day is for my own satisfaction. I applaud my efforts knowing that my achievements don't give me value; they are just what I do.

214. Reality isn't happening to us; we are happening to reality.

I will no longer be a victim of circumstances because that is impossible. It is my choice how I feel, what I do, and what I create in my life experiences. I see my reality as having everything I imagine perfection is.

---

215. Sometimes having too much good sense is restrictive. Do something impulsive today and don't worry about the consequences.

Stop. Don't think. Do.

216. We only worry about our relationships
with others when we are unsure of the
one we have with ourselves.

*When I bend to be what I think others want
me to be, I am no longer aware of who I am,
and they don't know the real me. Today I will
speak my mind with the words of my heart,
and act only upon what I feel is right for me.
I know that in spite of my fears I will be loved
and accepted just as I am.*

———————

217. Grass is beautiful when it grows upon
the earth, but when it grows around
our feet for too long, we can't move.

*I know that life isn't coming to me. Today I
will take a chance on something I had hesi-
tated to try. I will do my part to make my
dreams come alive, and they will no longer be
a secret.*

218. Peace of mind only requires letting it happen.

This day I will be still in my mind, trusting that all is perfection even when I can't tell the difference.

---

219. When desires and needs become confused, the needs remain unmet and the desires become only unfulfilled dreams. If we first realize, then meet, our true needs, all our dreams can become reality.

What I need sustains me. What I desire enhances me. Today I will give myself what I need without fail, and I will dream my reality beyond my needs and into all that I can imagine, willing to live it all with bliss.

220. We are created of all things and all things are created of us; therefore, there can be no thing and no one lesser or greater that us. We are an integrally woven part of the living One.

Today I will see others as mirrors of myself, recognizing what I love and what I want to change.

---

221. Honesty to self translates to truth in all directions.

When I am honest with me, there is nothing to defend and everything to gain.

222. We only get what we ask for. First, we have to ask. Second, we must believe that we deserve it, and third we must be willing to accept it.

Today I am willing to accept all that I have requested in the light, with gratitude and satisfaction.

———

223. Passion has many faces but compassion only one.

This day I will not look away from what makes me uncomfortable. Instead I will face it fully until I have no reason for discomfort.

224. Our perceptions determine our version of truth, not necessarily the reality of it.

This day, as I move through life, I will carefully consider how I feel, what I think I see and hear, as if I have a new set of eyes, interpreting everything from within all that surprises me, all that I have come to know with only positive perceptions, and not all of the voices who would tell me anything otherwise.

———

225. Regret means never having said you are sorry.

Today I will finish something that has bothered me for years. I will do or say whatever it takes to make amends even if it is to myself.

226. Greatness often doesn't recognize itself; it just is.

When I admire others today, I will acknowledge that what I admire about them are traits that I may have too. I am special as well, with other, unique gifts of my own that I may not have discovered yet, but I will.

———

227. Joy is a choice.

Today I celebrate that I am. I choose all things positive in every moment.

———

228. Meanness is manipulative.

When others are mean, or I witness meanness happening around me, I will recognize that those who are being mean really need something they don't know how to ask for kindly.

229

Our perceptions determine our version of truth, not necessarily the reality of it.

I know that not all of my perceptions are accurate and that if I give things a little time, I have the opportunity to realize the truth all around me.

230. Diligence doesn't mean staying so focused on our task that we miss everything else.

My life's purpose is not to achieve, but to love. I have complete faith that everything I have set as a goal is already a reality waiting to meet me in a specific moment in time. To get there, all I need to do is let go, live, and watch for the synchronicities along the way that tell me how to get there the fastest.

————

231. When something is out of truth, our bodies tell us before anything else does. We tense, hold our breath, feel it in our solar plexus. Maybe we should listen.

My body and I are in sync, at ease, relaxed, with no reason to defend. My body is my gauge for truth and I am listening.

232. The sacrifices we make are usually about someone else.

Today I will not rush to fix things for others. Instead I will observe with compassion that they have created for the expansion of their own experiences. As I observe, I will learn from everyone around me how not to do things the hard way.

———

233. The depth and amount of joy we experience are directly relative to how much we are willing to accept.

I openly accept and receive unlimited joy this day and every day forward.

234. Ignorance propagates illusion, destroys personal power, and fools no one except those who choose it.

I know that not looking doesn't make things better or make them go away; it just delays the discomfort of dealing with them, in fact, exacerbating my uneasiness; therefore, today I will ignore nothing, knowing what is mine to be responsible for, and what isn't.

---

235. More often than not wisdom is found in silence.

I need to say nothing to be recognized as wise or intelligent. As I embody who I am and what I learn along the way, my wisdom will speak for itself, and it has to impress no one.

236. Secrets are nothing more than control issues in action.

When I don't speak my truth, I don't get what I want or what I need. When others don't speak the truth, the secrets fester into conflict or worse. Today I will require that the truth be said whether it is mine or someone else's.

———

237. Conflicts cannot be resolved until the real root of the disagreement is recognized and both parties are willing to acknowledge it.

Most arguments and conflicts are about something in the past that recognizes an opportunity in a current situation to rear its injured head. Today, before engaging in conflict of any kind, I will make sure of what is really happening, and that there is a current conflict that needs to be battled at all.

238. We can't truly connect with each other until our defenses are out of the way and we act authentically.

Today my walls will come down, letting into me the beauty of others and mine to them. I will be authentic in every way.

---

239. Things don't just happen. For every action there is a reaction. We have to do our part toward the intended outcome.

This day I will live intentionally, realizing that everything I do, think, say, or mean comes alive as a future reality.

240. Peace requires broader perceptions in order for the infinite possibilities available to override the need to fight.

Today I won't be so quick to criticize or to assume that anything is as it seems. I will be open to possibilities that I had not yet considered that may change the entire picture.

---

241. Penance is what we do to make everyone else feel better about what we have done.

I will no longer punish myself for what others believe I have done. I will not chastise myself for what I may have done. Instead, I will learn from my experiences and do things differently next time.

242. To balance the body, mind, and spirit, believe, know, and let it be.

I believe that I am a perfect child of creation. I know that this is so. So be it.

---

243. Abundance is value. If we don't give ourselves the value we deserve, neither do we give ourselves the abundance we so desire.

I am priceless.

244. Embarrassment is nothing more than having a lack of humor about ourselves. When we have the ability to laugh first, the game is over and no damage is done.

Today I will laugh at my humanity sincerely and when I do, others will laugh with me.

———

245. Spiritually, we don't grow; we just remember.

There is so much within me that I don't yet know. If I just let myself be who I am, I will begin to remember all of the beauty that resides in me and that exquisiteness will begin to reflect all around me.

246. Tension is an indication of untruth. Ours internally, or ours in reaction to something externally, but always ours.

Today if I feel or sense tension, I will immediately look for the truth that lurks just beneath the surface of the situation.

---

247. Listen inward for it is there the truth resides.

Under all of the clutter of my thoughts is a truth so great it defies words.

---

248. Achievement means we must accomplish something to establish our value. Our value is already priceless and infinite. There is no need to prove anything to anyone.

There is nothing I need to do to be who I am; I already am.

249. Our divinity isn't some separate part of us; it is the driving force of our lives and the very breath of creation that animates every cell of our earthly being.

Today I know that I no longer need to seek my divinity; my link to all that is, for I am that, and it is me, and together we are One.

---

250. Building confidence only proves that we are still trying to fit in. The only reason we think we don't have it is because we listened to everyone else in the first place.

I know who I am and I have no need to prove that to anyone else. They have enough on their plates figuring out who they are.

251. Words mean nothing when used only to fill silence. They mean little else the rest of the time. It is what is behind them that really matters.

This day I won't fill the gaps with words; rather, I will listen carefully within those moments of silence for the great wisdom that is suspended there.

————

252. If yesterday we regret and tomorrow we worry about, today is our opportunity to heal the past and to set up a perfect future.

It is true that past, present, and future coincide with each other. Because of that, doing the best I can to live to my fullest with ease and grace will heal my past and prepare me for a future of everything that I desire.

253. There are many ways to take a journey. Traveling on one that plods along, never looking up, tending to every detail whether it matters or not, or the one that is joyfully taken, embracing the now simply for what it is and allowing each moment to reveal its magic. There is no baggage needed, simply the willingness to embark.

Today I will travel down a road I have never taken, I will choose to do something differently than I have in the past, I will talk with someone I have never met, all the while noticing that these changes have opened my life to entirely new possibilities.

254. Constancy refers to the fact that no matter what we do, or what others do, life goes on, and it is all small stuff in relation to the totality of the One.

In the circle of life, everything has a cycle. I realize that there will always be endings as well as new beginnings, and I am willing to embrace each as part of the fullness of my life.

---

255. Our innocence is that sweet spot inside of us that we developed all of our defenses to protect. It is also that place where our imagination still reigns and our hearts know no reason to be closed off. Finding our innocence is easy once we are willing to let down the walls and live out loud.

Today I relax all of my tension and allow myself to feel the child within me. I am willing to give my inner child whatever she needs to feel loved and safe, and if she wants to come out and play, I am game.

256. Infinite possibilities await you today, and the only thing you need to take advantage of them is to notice.

Today I will slow down and notice the beauty around me.

---

257. Brilliance is far more than intelligence. It is that part of us that shines when we live the truth and our hearts are on fire.

I no longer accept what pulls me down. Instead I embrace all that lifts me to my joy.

258. Beyond the money, what is the true cost of what you are after? Is it really worth it?

This day I will examine my true motivation for all of my circumstances, and if I find anything at all that I am not doing for my own greatest good, I will stop doing it.

———

259. In this now are you safe? Do you have everything that you need? Yes? Yes? Then what are you worrying about?

Today I celebrate that I AM, allowing all of my fear and worries to melt away, leaving only lightness in me.

260

Greatness is not determined by the world, but by a courageous choice made in a singular moment that changes the outcome forever.

I acknowledge that there are parts of me that are capable of greatness, and the fact that I am at all is a magnificent accomplishment, for I as a soul have found my way to life, to living, to loving, to . . . well, anything that I can imagine.

261. Our connection to the One is never lost but often ignored.

To separate myself from all else is not possible except by the way I see things. I choose to see my precious being as a vast contribution to all that is. In return, I also realize that Creation supports me in all that I am and do. I am loved beyond words.

---

262. If we live within reason, then we never experience why it was instilled upon us in the first place.

Today I leap out of my safety zone to experience the unlimited aspects of being a soul who has free will . . . for me; there are no boundaries except those I put in the way.

263. Expectations are disappointments smothered in secret desires.

Today I expect nothing and am open to everything. I will speak my heart with courage and ease.

———————

264. We don't have to achieve anything to be perfect; our perfection is inherent.

The fact that we have to achieve anything has been taught to us. Achievement doesn't make me who I am. It is who I am that achieves.

———————

265. Miracles are those events that we believe to be impossible. Believe in their possibility, and they may become commonplace.

Today I won't be disappointed in anything.

266. Life only works when we participate.

This day I won't let myself down.

———

267. Passion is love in action.

I will do what I love no matter what. I love so many things, my opportunities for expressing my heart are endless.

———

268. Our passion is not something we must find; it is everything that we love.

There is nothing I cannot love either for its beauty or for its pain.

269. Each moment is perfect and does not require comprehension, simply participation.

Today I won't force anything. I will let myself be comfortable to allow things to flow in their natural way, unfolding for me as constant revelations of who I am and all that comes to me.

———

270. Wisdom is not something that we learn, or can study for. It comes from applying living to the fineness of being.

Today I will not preach what I have come to know; instead I will embody it, becoming a glimmering light for all to encounter.

271. Our purpose isn't a singular achieve-ment, in fact, not an achievement at all. It is the totality of every moment that we live and breathe.

My purpose is every moment that I exist for, it is in each of these that gifts are exchanged between me and all that I encounter.

---

272. Aggression comes from limited per-ception that becomes so single minded that no other reality is possible in that now.

I don't have to be aggressive to get what I want. I know that true power is gentle power, the power of my heart.

273. Wanting something too badly compresses the energy of the one who desires until the wanted thing cannot possibly exist.

I realize that desperation only brings disappointment. Today I will reassess my needs and find the truth of them, letting all else go as frivolity of my mind.

———

274. Peace is only found when we no longer have the need to fight.

I don't have to give up or give in to win. Instead, I choose not to conflict or resist at all, but rather to participate willingly in whatever comes.

275. Reality is nothing more than our beliefs becoming our experience.

My beliefs are the result of my mind's need to make all of my experiences make sense. I choose to know that I am not my beliefs, but instead the Master of my being.

———

276. Lightning takes place on both ends of the storm. There is always stillness at the center.

Today I will find the center of my being, there where the stillness resides. I will become that, allowing all else to flow by me in its natural course.

277

What was no longer matters. It is what we do with it that does.

I know when I carry my regrets around, refusing to let go of them, my life becomes heavier with each regret, and I trust less all of the time. Instead of regrets, I choose to trust that I know what is best for me, and I celebrate all of my experiences for helping me to be who I am in this now.

278. Stillness is movement at rest.

As I am still I cannot help but notice . . . me.

---

279. No one can give us freedom. If freedom seems to come from outside of us,
what appears to be freedom may be the
door to a cage that locks behind us.

*I am the Master of all that I am and all that
I do. By choosing my own Mastery, I can no
longer be the victim of anyone else's idea of
who I am or must be.*

---

280. Our secret desires need not be secret.
It is better to live them loudly than to
always wonder why we didn't.

*If I don't tell people what I want, I will never
get what I asked for.*

281. Your body does exactly as it is told.

> *My body is healthy and well, whole and com-plete. No matter what past experiences it may have had, my body reflects the perfection that I am now.*

---

282. Being spiritual doesn't mean that you have to lack or do without. Quite the contrary. Being spiritual means giv-ing yourself enough value to have and receive everything that you need. You are priceless.

> *I gratefully accept all of the abundance that my divinity provides to me.*

283. Every large, overwhelming circumstance is comprised of nothing but
small parts that when unraveled were
really nothing at all.

*No matter what my first impression may be, it
is all small stuff. I am willing to look again so
that I don't miss something wonderful.*

---

284. Guilt is never having said you are
sorry.

*I am responsible for all of my actions, percep-
tions, feelings, and more. Today I will make
amends for all that I have blamed others for.*

285. Unconditionality is acceptance of others no matter what and loving them in spite of perceived differences.

Today I will notice something that I love about everyone I encounter. If I don't see it at first, I will look more carefully for the light that I know is there.

———

286. Our destiny isn't written in concrete; it is chosen by us one moment at a time.

I know that if I don't like how things have turned out, all that I need to do is choose again.

———

287. Infinite possibilities await the moment that we conceive them.

I have the ability to imagine and therefore am unlimited in what I can create.

288. Sense is what is left when the fear subsides.

Fear is a version of insanity, for it is in no way based in reality.

————

289. Integrity is far more than telling the truth. It is living it.

This day I am honest with myself first and secondly with all others. As I am, I am at ease, for there remains nothing within me to defend. I am free.

————

290. You can prove your point by not need-ing to.

I have to convince no one of what I mean even if I don't yet understand it myself.

291. What we love in others are the things we find inaccessible in ourselves.

Today I acknowledge that what I love about someone else is just a part of me that I have denied being. Now that I am aware of it, I choose to reflect the traits that I love as my own.

———

292. Speak what you really mean and there won't be any question about what you meant.

When I speak my truth with love, I can't help being heard. As I am, those around me will respond with the same respect I have given them.

293. Time is a control issue.

I cannot control what is not mine to hold.

––––––––

294. Immense: How huge our problems seem when we don't deal with them. The truth is that they remain just as small and it is our emotions that grow because we feed them with our fear, immobilized by our very selves.

Today if I feel paralyzed or ineffectual I will first breathe, then look again at the situation realizing that what I am really feeling is hesitance to act upon something I don't yet understand. I am willing to consider whatever it is I need to comprehend so that I may act on it with dignity and grace.

295. One cannot be gentle to others without reserve unless one has first learned to be gentle with one's self.

This day I honor myself with gentleness and care. I will not do anything I don't want to, and I won't rush to do things for others when my own life tasks are left undone.

---

296. Don't work on anything; just do it.

I accept that all that I do can be easy depending upon how I go about it. I choose not to be overwhelmed today.

297. Complexity is merely an entanglement of simplicities.

I have the ability to sort through complexities without becoming emotionally over extended so that I can find the simple truth buried inside.

---

298. What is beautiful in the world is a reflection of your heart shining back at you.

I know that I am beautiful no matter what, and when I see myself any other way that is because I have forgotten to see me with my own eyes.

299. Adversity is all about only having the outcome your way.

Today I am open to consider every possibility that comes to me even when a new possibility may be something out of my life experience or comfort zone.

---

300. Remember that in all of your giving you are only filled and full when you learn to receive equally.

I open my hands, my arms, and my heart to receive all that comes to me with ease and grace, and I am grateful for it.

301. That which you desire has always been yours unless by your doubts you denied it.

I know that everything I desire is not subject to anyone's approval.

———

302. An uphill climb is only hard when you keep looking up to see how far you have to go.

Today I won't concentrate so hard on my tasks that they become drudgery. Instead, I will joyfully move through my day, remaining in the now, appreciating the benefits of all my efforts.

303. How we react to others is no one else's fault.

This day I will be kind in every moment, even when I don't feel like it.

———

304. Peace only reigns when our inner battles cease.

I trust that my soul knows its way through this life, that all I need to do is choose at the crossroads, and that all struggles are really self-imposed. Therefore, my journey will be in peace.

———

305. Brilliance has nothing to do with intelligence and everything to do with how we shine our inner light.

I have to be nothing to be brilliant except to be who I am, and I will shine radiantly as me with no need for embellishment.

306. Imagination is the impetus to all reality.

I have the ability to imagine; therefore my possibilities are unlimited.

————

307. A fire in the heart releases the dam of drowning perspectives.

Today I ignite the fire within me, that which comes from true bliss, and the very luminosity of my heart will extinguish all that would keep me from my own light.

————

308. Loss creates a space for whatever fullness comes next.

I have grieved and now I choose to become full again, for there is room in my heart for what can be, and a permanent place for what has been. The depths of my love are endless.

309. How much depth we experience in life depends entirely upon how deep we are willing to go.

I choose to no longer monitor or limit myself because I deserve to have it all.

———

310. To be open does not mean to be raw and exposed; it means to be an authentic vessel willing to receive whatever gifts life has to offer.

Today I will reveal what is in my heart.

311. Unconditionality is a state of being, not a way of being.

If I judge myself and not others, I am still conditional. I choose this day to let go of all forms of judgment especially of my self and to see others and me as who we really are.

———

312. There are no mistakes, only opportunities to become aware, change direction, or learn the depths that we might have previously avoided.

Today if I don't like the results of my decisions, I know that I have the right and the power to choose again.

313. There are many ways to bleed. It is those injuries we can't see that often fester unattended.

My pain is not my identity; it is my impetus to find my joy.

———

314. When we worry, it is as if we have leaned forward out of our bodies looking into the future for something to go wrong.

This day I will stay firmly in my body knowing that everything I need is now and that what might be is my imagination, not real truth.

315. The difference between fantasy and reality is whether or not you act.

Today instead of saying, "What if?" I will say, "Why not?"

---

316. To belittle is to be little, the child seeking false power.

I will not criticize others because they show me exactly what I fear about myself. Instead I will have compassion for them because there by the grace of creation goes me.

---

317. To unravel the mysteries, you must simply accept that they exist.

I believe in the impossible. I believe in magic. I believe in miracles!

318. True love isn't like a Hallmark card. It is a state of unconditional being that radiates from our center, our heart of hearts, outward to everything and everyone we encounter and is willing to accept the same in return.

I AM the love I desire.

---

319. What is infinite is everything we have not defined. Within that infinite resides all of the possibilities that we had missed by our defining.

I don't need to know anything because I am everything. Today I will just go with the flow and see where it takes me.

---

320. You are defined only by the variations of truth that you tell yourself.

I am not what others say I am. I am who I know I am.

321. Magic only happens when we let it.

I believe in the magic that I know comes when I am not looking for it . . . and I love surprises!

———

322. The ultimate satisfaction is not needing to be satisfied.

If I need to be satisfied that isn't enough. I choose to be fulfilled!

———

323. Your greatest depths of pain hold the key to your highest pinnacles of compassion.

My pain is not my detriment; it is my guide to the greatest depths so that I can find my joy.

324. There are no mistakes, only choices made. To change course, choose again!

Today I will choose a different course to everything that I desire, and it will be exactly what I needed.

———

325. Where is your attention? Wherever it is so is your power.

Today I will not be distracted by anything that takes me away from where I mean to be.

———

326. The only approval you need, ever, is your own.

This day the committee in my head will be silent. The voices from my past have no business in my now. I am free of them.

327. You cannot let go of that which you have not owned.

I accept my part in everything I experience. No one is responsible for how I feel but me.

---

328. Your life purpose isn't a singular event for you to achieve; rather, it is every moment that you exist and how you live each one.

As I move through this day I know that I am exchanging with everything and everyone around me. I choose to take on only the greatest of all my experiences so that I receive only that which I meant to have.

---

329. To nourish your soul is to embrace your divinity.

Today I will do something just for me and I won't feel guilty.

330. To heal one's self takes more than just believing. It takes knowing that it is done.

There is nothing wrong with me because I can be nothing less than perfect.

---

331. What is known and unknown is all the same. It is how you see it that makes the difference. There is nothing more exquisite than a heart and soul expressing its deepest creative being, mindless of the outcome.

I already know that if I have imagined anything it is already a reality. Knowing that, I have the freedom to be open to all of the possibilities that can make my coming reality far more perfect than I could have imagined.

332. Draw upon the infinite to define life.

I know that in my creative process there are details I might not consider so I am leaving those details to the heavens, and all I need to do is accept them as gifts from me to myself.

---

333. When you create from anything out-side of yourself, you become a victim of your own creative process.

Today I will look to no one to give me anything. I know that everything comes from first my imagining, next my intention, and third my willingness to accept what I have created.

334. You have the power to change your life right now.

Today I will change whatever isn't working for me and I won't be afraid.

––––––––

335. Asking indicates that you do not believe in what you intend. Command life.

This day I command the forces of creation to bring me whatever I desire and to keep me sustained in the process.

––––––––

336. All forms of unconditionality travel with ease and grace.

Today I accept even what I don't understand.

337. Recognize the value of your value.

I am precious and because of that I am priceless.

―――――――

338. Fear causes paralysis of one's natural progression.

I have no reason to fear anything for I am capable of everything.

―――――――

339. It is not the power that is unsafe, but the perception of not having it . . .

There is no external power that is greater than my own.

340. We cannot do what we do not.

Today I will do whatever it takes to avoid future regret.

———

341. You do not have to give yourself per-mission to be who you are. Just accept that it is so.

I AM, therefore I CAN.

———

342. Change forces choice but change is a choice.

I choose to change all that does not serve me, no longer living for others at my expense.

343. The only limits we have are those which are self-imposed.

Today I release all of my perceived limitations.

————

344. Questions cannot be answered until we live them.

I realize that the answers I seek may not be readily available so I am willing to keep going until all of my questions become answers and I become them too.

————

345. That which you seek also seeks you.

I know that whatever I am looking for is already something that I have created for another now.

346

When pure heart meets with pureness of being, in all its innocence is born an existence of harmony with all things.

I don't need to make things complex for them to be okay. By realizing that all complexity comes from my resistance to go there in the first place, I can become what I never imagined I could.

347. Each time that you interact with another, and each time they with you, there is an exchange of energies that changes each of you forever. That which you have given to them, and that which you have received, changes your energetic structure in that moment and theirs as well. You may never know how you have affected others in brief passing. Know that in a much more subtle yet grander way, you may have changed their life completely.

Today I choose to give the authentic gift of me, and accept nothing that is untrue, only that which sustains, comforts, bolsters, and enhances me.

———

348. To seek with your mind is to attempt to quantify that which is immeasurable.

I don't need to know; I just need to be who I am and that is good enough.

349. It is much easier to act from faith than from fear.

I accept and believe that whatever I know to be true will never, ever let me down.

───────

350. We are filled by our own grace, never that of another.

I am filled with the light of creation, and because of that, there is no room within me for lack.

351. Coincidence is nothing less than a pre-ordained event eloquently choreographed in perfect relation with all other events in the Universe so that at the very moment of its occurrence it is perfect.

Today I will recognize that every coincidence is a synchronicity leading me to exactly where I want to be.

---

352. Being loose in your existence assures you a snug fit in the scheme of things.

Today I will hold onto nothing. I don't need to be in control. I am divinely guided.

353. You are already perfect. To know this is perfection.

I have nothing to prove to anyone anywhere.

———

354. To walk in a state of love is to touch everything with grace.

I realize that when I embody love I am contagious.

———

355. There are no impossibilities, and our options are limitless.

Today I am filled with so many choices that whatever I choose will be an exquisite reflection of what I meant it to be.

356. Nothing within you ever changes without your participation.

Today I let go of all my resistance.

———

357. Coincidence is merely a truth knocking at your consciousness.

I am a living synchronicity, always in the right place at the right time doing whatever is right for me.

———

358. Opposites attract because when mirrored, there exists an infinite reflection of their wholeness.

I realize that all conflict arises from me resisting anything I don't understand, so I am willing to be open to new possibilities even when they seem too big for me.

359. Freedom is what we get when we stop holding back.

Today I choose to be free of all that encumbers me.

———

360. Our real power is that we have the option to create from our own free will, of the infinite possibilities that are available to us.

I command the forces of change to bring me whatever is perfect for me in this now.

———

361. The intention of an investment is to benefit you in the future. How are your thoughts, words, and actions today going to benefit you later?

Today I will only invest my energy in the kind of future I want. I refuse to waver from my intended path.

362. Some disasters are just doors slamming firmly shut so that we can look toward something different.

When I see that a door is closing for me, I will not grieve. I will instead bravely walk in whatever direction another one is opening, and I won't look back.

———

363. Passion has many faces but compassion only one.

This day my heart is completely open, knowing that I will receive far more than I give, and I will give all that I am.

———

364. There is never an end, only a completion so that there is room for something new and different.

Today I will finish what hangs out there bothering me so that my attention can go to what I really want to be doing.

365

We are not what we do. In any given moment we are the perfect expression of our life's work.

I am an evolving being, shining the light of all my experiences, embodied wisdom gained from a lifetime of learning. I am everything that I have ever been, maturing, evolving, expressing, and being, everything that I can be, and I am divine.